YOUR VICTORIAN

omework Helper

by Louise Armstrong

Consultant: Alison Howard

How to use this book

Each topic in this book is clearly labelled and contains all these components:

Topic heading

Introduction to the topic

Sub-topic 1 offers complete information about one aspect of the topic

Choose a word from the Keyword Contents on page 3. Then, turn to the correct page and look for your word in BOLD CAPITALS. This will take you straight to the information you need

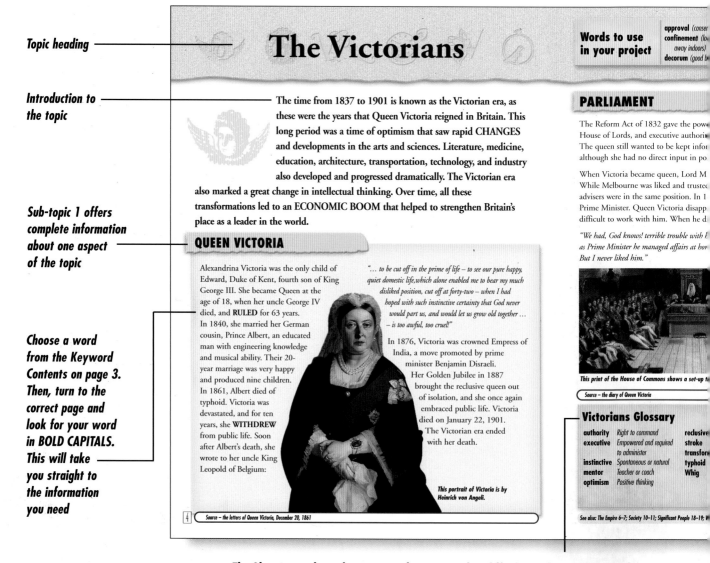

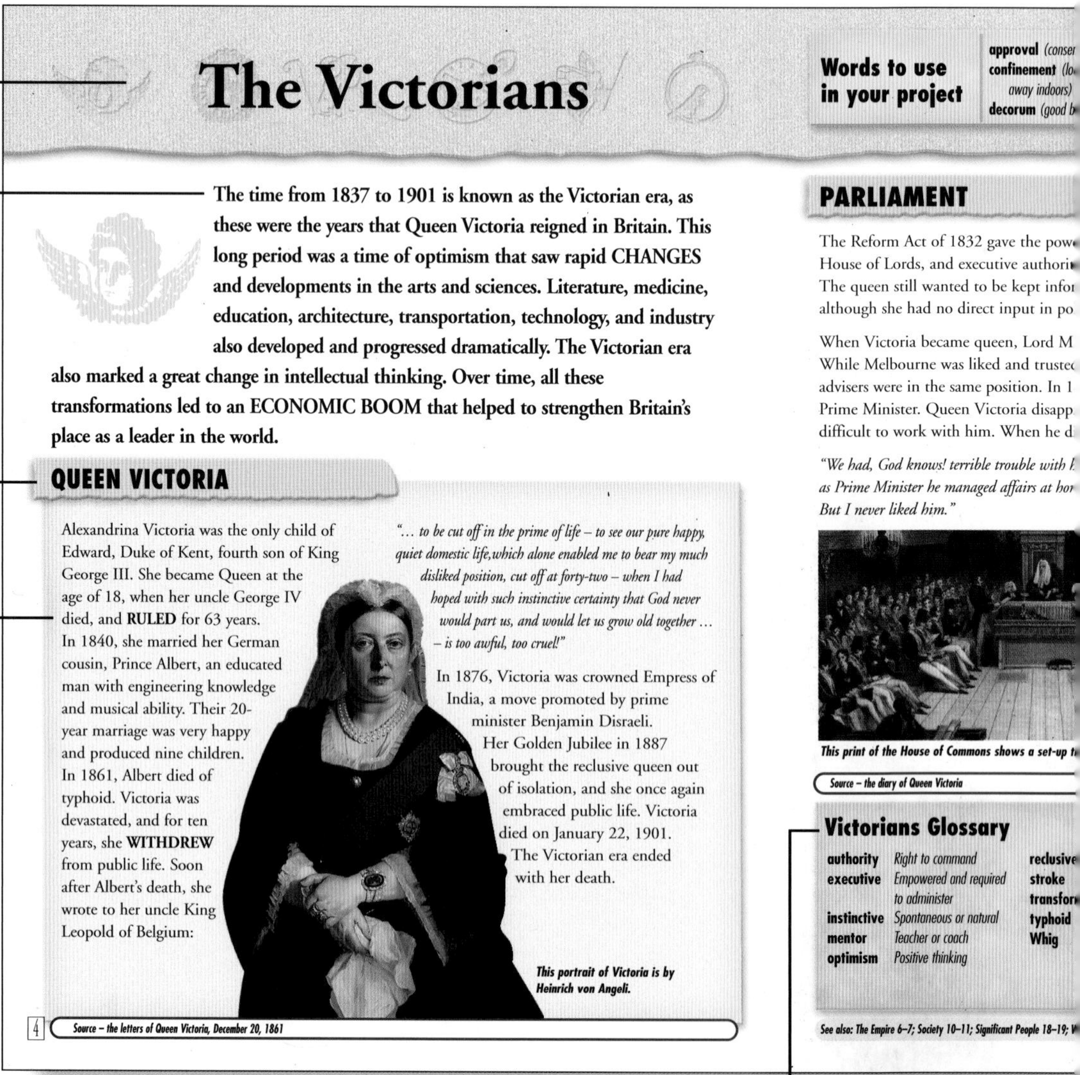

The Victorians

Words to use in your project

approval *(conser*
confinement *(lo*
away indoors)
decorum *(good b*

The time from 1837 to 1901 is known as the Victorian era, as these were the years that Queen Victoria reigned in Britain. This long period was a time of optimism that saw rapid CHANGES and developments in the arts and sciences. Literature, medicine, education, architecture, transportation, technology, and industry also developed and progressed dramatically. The Victorian era also marked a great change in intellectual thinking. Over time, all these transformations led to an ECONOMIC BOOM that helped to strengthen Britain's place as a leader in the world.

QUEEN VICTORIA

Alexandrina Victoria was the only child of Edward, Duke of Kent, fourth son of King George III. She became Queen at the age of 18, when her uncle George IV died, and **RULED** for 63 years. In 1840, she married her German cousin, Prince Albert, an educated man with engineering knowledge and musical ability. Their 20-year marriage was very happy and produced nine children. In 1861, Albert died of typhoid. Victoria was devastated, and for ten years, she **WITHDREW** from public life. Soon after Albert's death, she wrote to her uncle King Leopold of Belgium:

"... to be cut off in the prime of life – to see our pure happy, quiet domestic life,which alone enabled me to bear my much disliked position, cut off at forty-two – when I had hoped with such instinctive certainty that God never would part us, and would let us grow old together ... – is too awful, too cruel!"

In 1876, Victoria was crowned Empress of India, a move promoted by prime minister Benjamin Disraeli. Her Golden Jubilee in 1887 brought the reclusive queen out of isolation, and she once again embraced public life. Victoria died on January 22, 1901. The Victorian era ended with her death.

This portrait of Victoria is by Heinrich von Angeli.

4 Source – the letters of Queen Victoria, December 20, 1861

PARLIAMENT

The Reform Act of 1832 gave the pow
House of Lords, and executive authori
The queen still wanted to be kept infor
although she had no direct input in po

When Victoria became queen, Lord M
While Melbourne was liked and truste
advisers were in the same position. In 1
Prime Minister. Queen Victoria disapp
difficult to work with him. When he d

"We had, God knows! terrible trouble with l
as Prime Minister he managed affairs at hor
But I never liked him."

This print of the House of Commons shows a set-up t

Source – the diary of Queen Victoria

Victorians Glossary

authority	*Right to command*	**reclusive**
executive	*Empowered and required to administer*	**stroke**
		transfor
instinctive	*Spontaneous or natural*	**typhoid**
mentor	*Teacher or coach*	**Whig**
optimism	*Positive thinking*	

See also: The Empire 6–7; Society 10–11; Significant People 18–19;

The Glossary explains the meaning of any unusual or difficult words appearing on these two pages

First published in Great Britain in 2005 by ***ticktock*** Media Ltd.,
Unit 2, Orchard Business Centre, North Farm Road, Tunbridge Wells, Kent, TN2 3XF
We would like to thank: Book Matrix Ltd for their help with this book.
ISBN 1 86007 829 X
Printed in China
A CIP catalogue record for this book is available from the British Library.

Sub-topic 2 offers complete information about one aspect of the topic

Some suggested words to use in your project

The Case Study is a closer look at a famous person, artefact or building that relates to the topic

Captions clearly explain what is in the picture

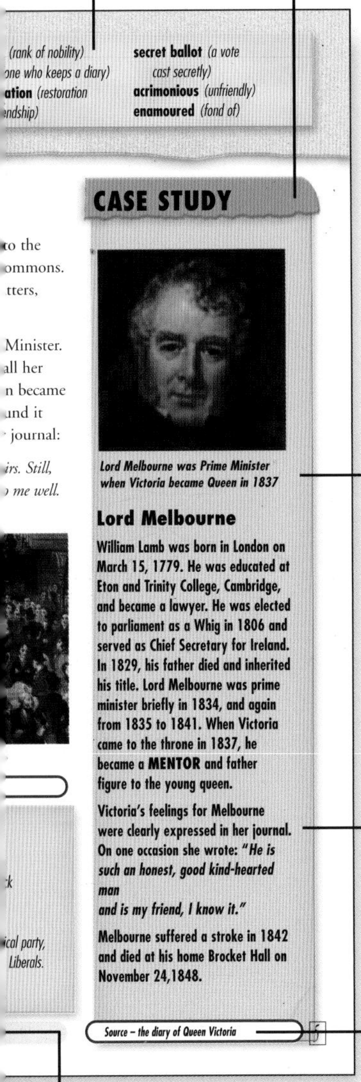

(rank of nobility)
one who keeps a diary)
ation (restoration
endship)
secret ballot (a vote cast secretly)
acrimonious (unfriendly)
enamoured (fond of)
to the
ommons.
tters,
Minister.
all her
n became
and it
journal:
irs. Still,
me well.
ical party,
Liberals.
CASE STUDY
Lord Melbourne was Prime Minister when Victoria became Queen in 1837
Lord Melbourne
William Lamb was born in London on March 15, 1779. He was educated at Eton and Trinity College, Cambridge, and became a lawyer. He was elected to parliament as a Whig in 1806 and served as Chief Secretary for Ireland. In 1829, his father died and inherited his title. Lord Melbourne was prime minister briefly in 1834, and again from 1835 to 1841. When Victoria came to the throne in 1837, he became a MENTOR and father figure to the young queen.
Victoria's feelings for Melbourne were clearly expressed in her journal. On one occasion she wrote: "He is such an honest, good kind-hearted man and is my friend, I know it."
Melbourne suffered a stroke in 1842 and died at his home Brocket Hall on November 24,1848.
Source – the diary of Queen Victoria

Each photo or illustration is described and discussed in its accompanying text

Other pages in the book that relate to what you have read here are listed in this bar

At the bottom of some sections, a reference bar tells you where the quote has come from

Keyword Contents

The Victorians

Queen Victoria reigned in Britain from 1837 to 1901, so these years are known as the Victorian era. This long period was a time of optimism that saw rapid CHANGES and developments in the arts and sciences. Literature, medicine, education, architecture, transportation, technology, and industry also developed and progressed dramatically. The Victorian era also marked a great change in intellectual thinking. Over time, all these transformations led to an ECONOMIC BOOM that helped to strengthen Britain's place as a leader in the world.

QUEEN VICTORIA

Alexandrina Victoria was the only child of Edward, Duke of Kent, fourth son of King George III. She became Queen at the age of 18, when her uncle George IV died, and **RULED** for 63 years. In 1840, she married her German cousin, Prince Albert, an educated man with engineering knowledge and musical ability. Their 20-year marriage was very happy and produced nine children. In 1861, Albert died of typhoid. Victoria was devastated, and for ten years, she **WITHDREW** from public life. Soon after Albert's death, she wrote to her uncle King Leopold of Belgium:

"... to be cut off in the prime of life – to see our pure happy, quiet domestic life,which alone enabled me to bear my much disliked position, cut off at forty-two – when I had hoped with such instinctive certainty that God never would part us, and would let us grow old together ... – is too awful, too cruel!"

In 1876, Victoria was crowned Empress of India, a move promoted by prime minister Benjamin Disraeli. Her Golden Jubilee in 1887 brought the reclusive queen out of isolation, and she once again embraced public life. Victoria died on January 22, 1901. The Victorian era ended with her death.

This portrait of Victoria is by Heinrich von Angeli.

Source – the letters of Queen Victoria, December 20, 1861

Words to use in your project

approval *(consent)*
confinement *(locked away indoors)*
decorum *(good behaviour)*
peerage *(rank of nobility)*
diarist *(one who keeps a diary)*
reconciliation *(restoration to friendship)*
secret ballot *(a vote cast secretly)*
acrimonious *(unfriendly)*
enamoured *(fond of)*

PARLIAMENT

The Reform Act of 1832 gave the power of making **LAWS** to the House of Lords, and executive authority to the House of Commons. The queen still wanted to be kept informed on political matters, although she had no direct input in policy decisions.

When Victoria became queen, Lord Melbourne was Prime Minister. While Melbourne was liked and trusted by the queen, not all her advisers were in the same position. In 1855, Lord Palmerston became Prime Minister. Queen Victoria disapproved of him and found it difficult to work with him. When he died, she wrote in her journal:

"We had, God knows! terrible trouble with him about Foreign Affairs. Still, as Prime Minister he managed affairs at home well, and behaved to me well. But I never liked him."

This print of the House of Commons shows a set-up that is much the same today.

Source – the diary of Queen Victoria

Victorians Glossary

authority Right to command
executive Empowered and required to administer
instinctive Spontaneous or natural
mentor Teacher or coach
optimism Positive thinking
reclusive Living quietly
stroke Sudden heart attack
transformation Process of change
typhoid Infectious fever
Whig Member of a political party, rather like modern Liberals.

See also: The Empire 6–7; Society 10–11; Significant People 18–19; Work and Leisure 24–25

CASE STUDY

Lord Melbourne was Prime Minister when Victoria became Queen in 1837.

Lord Melbourne

William Lamb was born in London on March 15, 1779. He was educated at Eton and Trinity College, Cambridge, and became a lawyer. He was elected to parliament as a Whig in 1806 and served as Chief Secretary for Ireland. In 1829, his father died and inherited his title. Lord Melbourne was prime minister briefly in 1834, and again from 1835 to 1841. When Victoria came to the throne in 1837, he became a MENTOR and father figure to the young queen.

Victoria's feelings for Melbourne were clearly expressed in her journal. On one occasion she wrote: *"He is such an honest, good kind-hearted man and is my friend, I know it."*

Melbourne suffered a stroke in 1842 and died at his home Brocket Hall on November 24,1848.

Source – the diary of Queen Victoria

The Empire

Under Queen Victoria, Britain became a richer, stronger, and more powerful country. The British Empire reached its zenith during her reign, and many people believe that England was at its best during Victorian times. British technology, COMMERCE, language and government spread throughout the British Empire, which covered roughly a quarter of the world's area and population. The development of the British COLONIES aided her extraordinary economic growth and helped to make Britain a world power.

EXPANSION

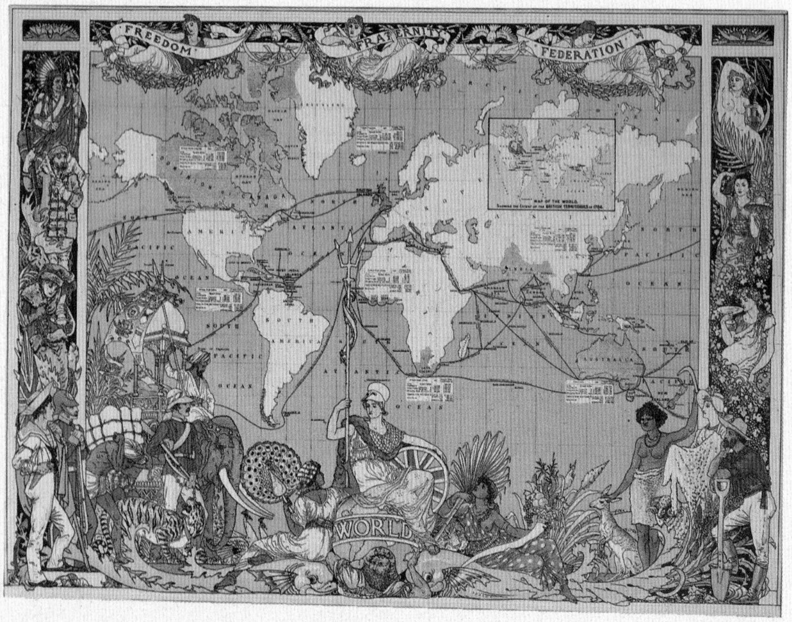

This map shows the extent of the British Empire (coloured orange) in 1886.

The British Empire was built over 300 years, but was at its height during the reign of Victoria. England **CONQUERED** many countries, including Egypt in 1881, Canada in 1867 and India in 1876. India was known as 'the Jewel in the Crown' of the British Empire. Central Africa and parts of Asia were added to

Britain's **ACQUISITIONS**. Many Victorians opposed imperialism because they saw it as **OPPRESSIVE** to the cultures of acquired countries, but British statesman Earl Grey believed the Empire was the best hope for the civilization of the world. In 1853 he wrote:

"I conceive that, by the acquisition of its colonial dominions, the Nation has incurred a responsibility of the highest kind. The authority of the British crown is at this moment the most powerful instrument, under Providence, of maintaining peace and order in many extensive regions of the earth, and thereby assists in diffusing amongst millions of the human race, the blessing of Christianity and civilization."

Source – Earl Grey, The Colonial Policy of Lord John Russell's Administration (1853).

Words to use in your project

conservatism *(traditional nature of something)*
constitutional *(way of ruling a state by a set of principles)*
evolve *(change naturally)*
indomitable *(impossible to subdue or defeat)*
legislation *(law)*
liberalism *(open-mindedness)*
seclusion *(isolation)*

INDUSTRIALISATION

Britain's industrial revolution reached its height during the Victorian era. It quickly became a country of industrialised towns, factories, mines and workshops. By 1900, 80 per cent of the population lived in cities. The massive **MIGRATION** to cities and towns caused the rise of slums and cramped housing.

Historian and social reformer Arnold Toynbee said:

"... the industrial England of to-day is not only one of external conditions. Side by side with the revolution which the intervening century has affected in the methods and organisation of production, there has taken place a change no less radical in men's economic principles, and in the attitude of the State to individual enterprise..."

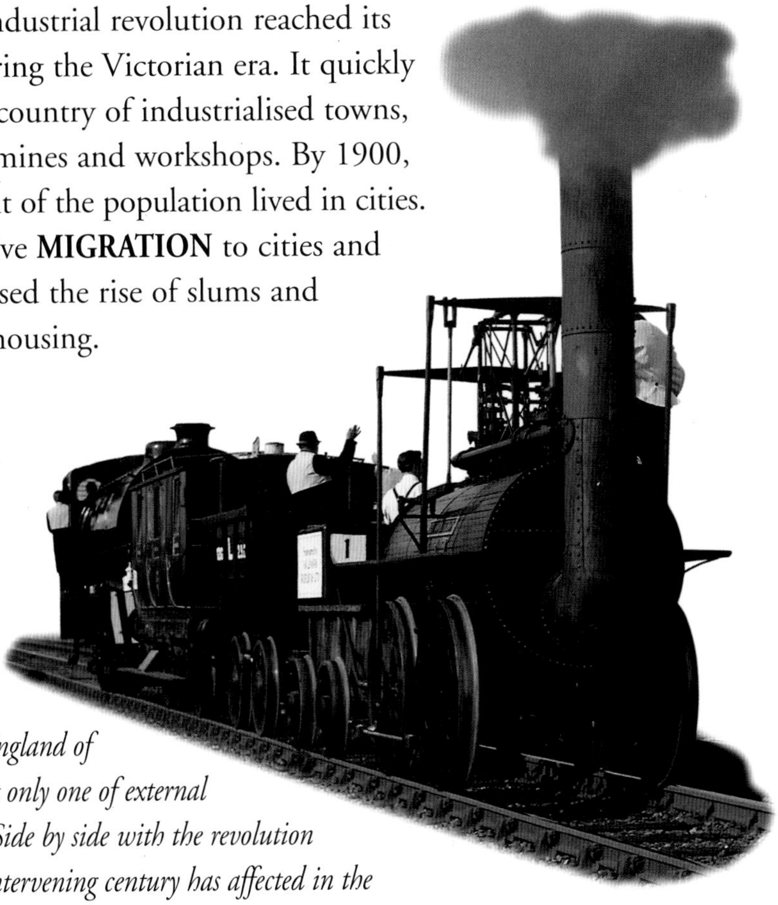

Rail travel began during the Industrial Revolution, and increased dramatically in the Victorian era.

Source – *Arnold Toynbee,* The Industrial Revolution in England *(1884).*

The Empire Glossary

acquisition	*Possession, taking ownership*
dominion	*Power or authority*
economic	*Relating to financial matters*
expansion	*Extension or development*
imperial	*Relating to an empire*
industries	*Businesses that make or produce things*
metropolis	*Large, busy city*
revolution	*Complete change*
zenith	*Highest point*

See also: Victorians 4–5; Religion 8–9; Literature 14–15; At Home 28–29

CASE STUDY

Victorian London

London was a city of startling contrasts. The population grew rapidly in the 19th century to more than six million. New building and development were set against overcrowded slums where people lived in appalling conditions.

Describing London in *The Morning Chronicle*, Henry Mayhew said: *"... the metropolis covered an extent of nearly 45,000 acres, and contained upwards of two hundred and sixty thousand houses, occupied by one million eight hundred and twenty thousand souls, constituting not only the densest, but the busiest hive, the most wondrous workshop, and the richest bank in the world."*

The River Thames, the hub of the British Empire, was clogged with **SHIPS** from all over the world, and London had more shipyards than anywhere on the globe.

View over the Houses of Parliament and the Thames in Victorian times.

Source – *The Morning Chronicle, October 19 1849.*

Religion

The Victorian era brought numerous challenges to Christianity. These included criticism of the BIBLE by supporters of evolutionary theories, including Charles Darwin, and many new sects of Christianity developing. The urban population expanded during Victorian times, and new chapels and CHURCHES were built, for both Catholics and for different Protestant sects. Many MISSIONARIES were sent to the various British colonies, with the aim of converting local people to Christianity.

CHRISTIAN VALUES

For rich and poor alike, the church was the centre of English life, but the dominance of the Church of England led to dissenting groups. New sects of Protestant faith were created by the wealthy and powerful middle class who wanted to combine their work ethic with Christian values. The principal religious groups of 19th-century England were Methodist, Baptist, Congregationalist, Unitarian and Quaker. While all these sects identified themselves as Christian, each had its own methods and interpretations of the Bible.

Victorians were appalled by Darwin's theory that man descended from apes.

Many religious sects felt that the only way to improve society was to convert everybody to their beliefs. Some people saw this as being hypocritical. The Church of England and other groups were professing to help the poor, while simply exploiting desperate people, imposing judgments and a sense of guilt that made their lives even more miserable. Charles Darwin wrote:

"If the misery of our poor be caused not by the laws of nature, but by our institutions, great is our sin."

Source – The Voyage of the Beagle, *Charles Darwin, 1839*

Words to use in your project

disillusioned *(relieved of beliefs)*
evangelist *(one who tries to convert others to Christianity)*
puritan *(person committed to morals and religion)*
theologians *(people who study religion)*

CHRISTIANITY

In Victorian England, religion was thought to be a remedy for all that was wrong with the world. The Church argued that if everyone accepted their view of Christianity, MORALITY would prevail and bring an end to crime, poverty and all types of abnormal behaviour. John Henry Newman, founder of the Oxford Movement, which wanted to bring the Anglican Church closer to Roman Catholicism, said:

"For thirty, forty, fifty years I have resisted to the best of my powers the spirit of liberalism in religion. Never did Holy Church need champions against it more sorely than now."

The Book of Common Prayer was used in all Anglican church services to ensure uniformity of practice and worship. Many new churches were built in urban areas to cater for the growing population. The most prominent feature of most churches was the bell tower, which was rung on Sunday for church services. Church attendance was highest in England's rural villages.

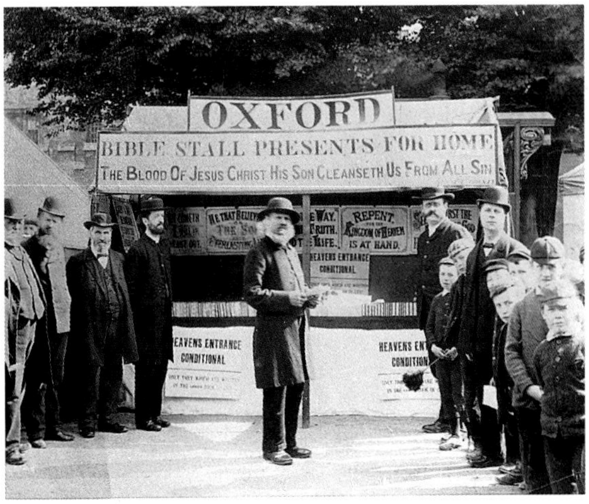

The Oxford Movement led the High Church campaign.

Source – John Henry Newman, speech, upon becoming a Cardinal, 1879

Religion Glossary

Anglican	*Church of England*
buttress	*Pillar of stone built against a wall*
convert	*Change religions*
dissent	*Disagree*
doctrines	*Beliefs or principles*
High Church	*Belief that the rituals of the Anglican church should be similar to those of the Roman Catholic Church*
masonry	*Stonework on a building*
profess	*Claim*
uniformity	*All the same*

See also: The Empire 6–7; Education 12–13; Architecture 16–17; Art and Craft 20–21

CASE STUDY

Westminster Abbey was extensively restored in the Victorian era.

Westminster Abbey

The Collegiate Church of St. Peter is also known as Westminster Abbey. Many royal **MARRIAGES** and funerals have taken place there, and it has been used as a **CORONATION** church since William the Conqueror was crowned there in 1066. Victoria was crowned at Westminster Abbey on June 28, 1838. In her diary on that day, she wrote:

"I reached the Abbey amid deafening cheers ... I was then seated upon St Edward's chair where the Dalmatic robe was clasped round me by the Lord Chamberlain...the Crown being placed on my head; which was, I must own, a beautiful, impressive moment.

During this era, Henry VII's Chapel and the Chapter House was restored. Much of the external masonry was refaced, and buttresses and pinnacles were reconstructed.

Source – The diary of Queen Victoria

Society

Victorian society was structured according to a system that divided people into classes: upper class, upper middle class, lower middle class and the working classes. Very poor people were the underclass. The upper class included the old aristocracy. The increasingly-powerful MIDDLE CLASSES protested against a society that rewarded inherited privilege, and strove to create a position for themselves. The working class included people across a wide range of occupations of varying STATUS and income. There was a large gap in status between skilled and unskilled workers.

UPPER AND MIDDLE CLASS

The 19th century was a time of great social change. Class divisions were marked by distinctions in dress, speech, social behaviour, and **ETIQUETTE**.

The upper class were the main employers and had the greatest wealth, which they exhibited at every opportunity, forever striving to extend their assets, from land and possessions to the number of servants they employed. The middle classes had great social and economic influence, and tried to copy the lifestyles of the upper class. They ranged from **LAWYERS**, doctors, factory owners, bankers and senior civil servants to shopkeepers, teachers and clerks. The working classes had a wide range of manual and service occupations.

William Makepeace Thackeray's novel *Vanity Fair* was presented as a work of fiction, but it was really about the moral decay and selfishness of Victorian society.

Thackeray felt that every level of society had been corrupted by capitalism and imperialism with their emphasis on wealth, rank, material goods, and ostentation. This is how he described one of his characters:

"Whenever he met a great man he grovelled before him as only a free-born Briton can do."

Wealth, possessions and a genteel lifestyle were important to the Victorians.

Source – Vanity Fair, William Makepeace Thackeray, 1847

Words to use in your project

affluent *(rich)*
courtesy *(politeness)*
destitution *(poverty)*
élite *(upper class)*
hierarchy *(class system)*
population explosion *(rapid growth in population)*
rookeries *(a crowded house)*
sewers *(drainage)*
starvation *(hunger)*
subsistence *(necessities of life)*

POOR AND WORKING CLASS

The working classes were powerful in terms of their vast numbers and because of greater recognition given to their value to society. The increased acceptance of the working classes led to the 1867 Reform Act, which extended the vote to more than 60 per cent of men.

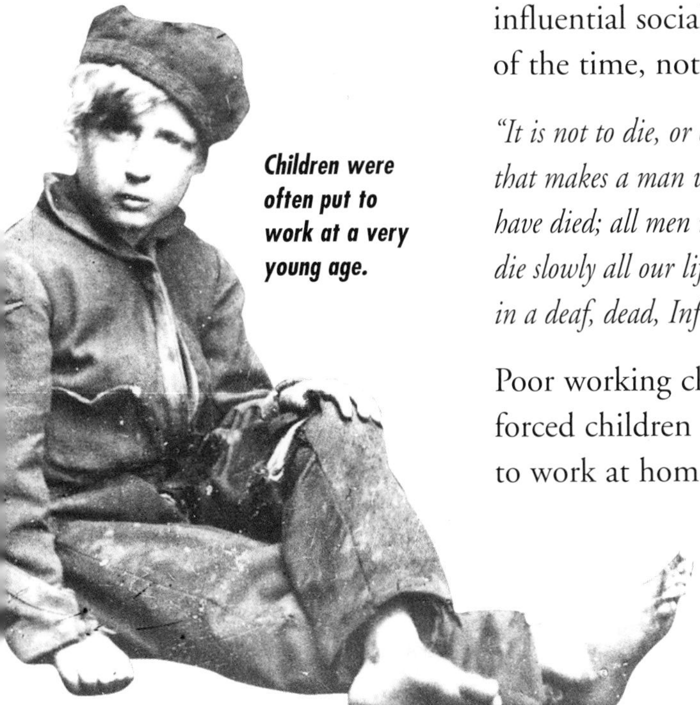

Children were often put to work at a very young age.

Despite the economic expansion of the Industrial Revolution, living conditions for the poor were **APPALLING**. Thomas Carlyle, one of the most influential social observers of the time, noted:

"It is not to die, or even to die of hunger, that makes a man wretched; many men have died; all men must die, … it is to die slowly all our life long, imprisoned in a deaf, dead, Infinite Injustice …"

Source – Past and Present Midas [The Condition of England] (1843), Thomas Carlyle

Poor working class parents often forced children as young as four to work at home. Although they earned only **PENNIES**, this was greatly needed to buy food and fuel.

Society Glossary

appalling	*Horrifying or shocking*
aristocracy	*Privileged class*
borough	*An area of local government*
etiquette	*Manner*
genteel	*Very polite*
grovel	*Make a big show of being unworthy*
influence	*Ability to change things*
inherited	*Passed on from parents or ancestors*
ostentation	*Showing off wealth*
unskilled	*Having no special training*
wretched	*Very unhappy or unfortunate state*

See also: Victorians 4–5; Education 12–13; Clothes and Jewellery 22–23; Health and Medicine 26–27

CASE STUDY

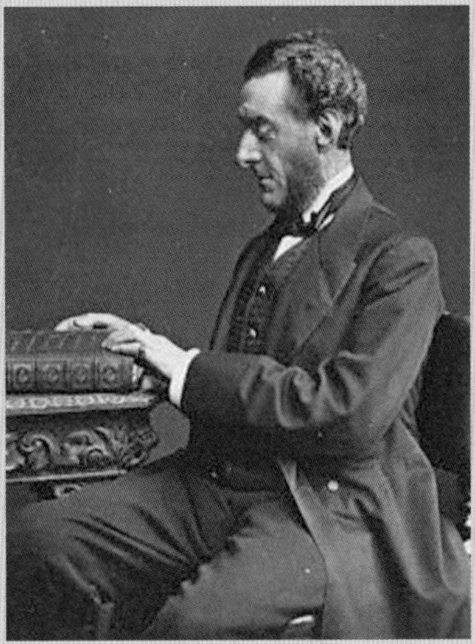

Anthony Ashley Cooper, 7th Earl of Shaftesbury.

Lord Shaftesbury

Anthony Ashley Cooper was elected member of parliament for Woodstock, a borough in Oxfordshire under the control of his family. He developed an interest in social issues after reading reports on child labour and became leader of the factory reform MOVEMENT. The 1833 Factory Act was passed by Parliament on his proposals. In 1840, he pushed through an act that prevented small boys being used as chimney sweeps. He also fought for a reduction in the hours that children worked in factories. He said:

"The future hopes of a country must, under God, be laid in the character and condition of its children; … My grand object is to bring these children within the reach of education."

Source – Lord Shaftesbury's speech to the House of Commons, August 4, 1840

Education

While wealthy children received education in many different subjects and skills, poor children might not receive any education at all. Upper-class children were often educated at home with a view to preparing them for UNIVERSITY. Middle-class children who were not taught at home usually went to private SCHOOLS. Working-class children attended schools which had usually one large classroom, with partitions that were used to divide the age groups and educational levels of students.

EDUCATION AT HOME

Governesses were women who taught upper- or middle-class children in their homes. Boys would sometimes be taught at home until the age of seven, when they were old enough to go to **BOARDING** school. Many governesses were quite well-educated, although the pay was low. The job was one of very few that were considered suitable for middle-class women who needed to earn a living. The position of governess could be very lonely. Although she had to have the education and manners of a lady, she was treated as a servant. However, other servants would generally not have much contact with her because she had a close relationship with the master's children.

Many young upper-class children were taught by their own mothers. Josephine Butler, who was born in 1828, tells of the experience in her autobiography:

"In the pre-educational era (for women at least), we had none of the advantages which girls of the present day have. We owed much to our dear mother, who was very firm in requiring from us that whatever we did should be thoroughly done..."

Children, whether they were educated at home or school, could be beaten if they did not learn their lessons.

Source – An Autobiographical Memoir, *Josephine Butler, 1913*

Words to use in your project

attendance *(presence)*
bourgeoisie *(the middle class)*
curriculum *(subjects taught in school)*
discipline *(strict rules; punishment)*
peers *(people of the same age)*
prospects *(expected outcome)*
stringent *(strict)*

SCHOOLS

Parents who had a little money to spare sent their children to school. Young children were often sent to dame schools, usually run by untrained women, while older children went to day school. Other schools were organised by churches and **CHARITIES**. Among these were the 'ragged' schools, attended by children from very poor families.

The school day typically lasted from 9am to 12.30pm and from 2pm to 4.30pm. Most of the children went home for dinner. Reading, writing and arithmetic were the core subjects taught at elementary schools.

Schooling had to be paid for throughout most of the 19th century, though more relaxed laws were later introduced. The 1870 Education Act stated:

"the country would be divided into about 2500 school districts;...own by-laws which would allow them to charge fees or, if they wanted, to let children in free."

A Victorian ragged school from the 1840s.

Source – Education Act of 1870

Education Glossary

autobiography	*Story of the author's life*
charity	*Organisation that work to help people*
dame	*Woman in authority*
elementary	*Primary*
era	*Period of time*
governess	*Female tutor*
logbook	*Record of events*
partitions	*An interior wall dividing one room from another*
ragged	*Shabby*
truants	*Children who miss classes*
vermin	*Pests such as head lice*

See also: Religion 8–9; Architecture 16–17; Significant People 18–19; Trade and Transport 30–31

CASE STUDY

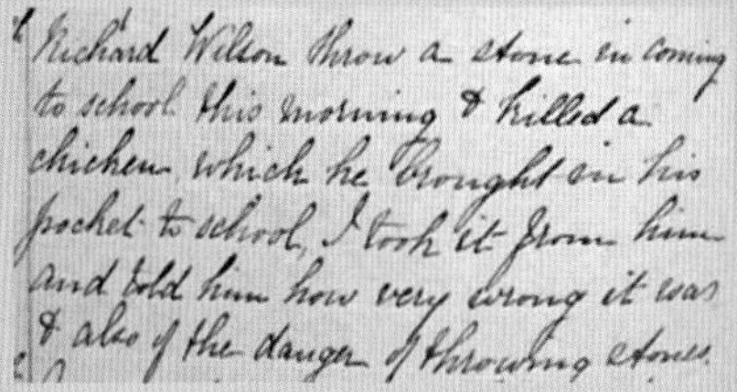

Richard Willon threw a stone in coming to school this morning & killed a chicken which he brought in his pocket to school, I took it from him and told him how very wrong it was & also of the danger of throwing stones

An entry from a Victorian school log book (1882).

Public School Log

Most schools kept a logbook to record PUNISHMENTS given to children and TEACHERS' comments. These extracts are from the log of Milton House Public School, Edinburgh in the late 19th century:

'April 8th

One death during week from Fever. Every member of Craig family ill with Fever and removed to hospital.

May 6th

Margaret Luke died on Monday (Class 6th)

May 13th

Universally large number of Truants. Parents of found summoned before the School Board tomorrow.

November 25th

Sent for Mrs Ferguson, New Street. Ordered her to take home her daughter and clean her head, which is overrun with vermin. This has escaped notice till now as the girl had a bandage over her head.'

Source – Milton House Public School Log, 1881

Literature

British writers produced some of their greatest literature during the 19th century. There was also a great rise in the number of people who were interested in reading everything from newspapers and magazines to the latest novel. The 19th century was also a time during which women came to be more readily accepted as NOVELISTS and poets. Most highly-regarded authors had received an upper-middle-class education. Poetry of the time was often lyrical and conformed to specific styles and structures.

POETRY

Many POETS of the Victorian age were concerned with exploring social, political and religious issues of the time in their work. The poetry of Robert Browning and his wife, Elizabeth Barrett Browning, was immensely popular, while that written by Rudyard Kipling captured the spirit of the lives of British soldiers during the expansion of the empire.

William Blake, Samuel Taylor Coleridge, William Wordsworth, Lord Byron and John Keats were among many poets who wrote in the ROMANTIC style.

Romanticism was a movement that flourished during the 19th century, and was advocated by poets, philosophers and artists. Romantic poets celebrated nature, feeling and the imagination in their work. Wordsworth explored many Romantic themes and ideas, as in the following example from one of his poems:

"The birds around me hopp'd and play'd
Their thought I cannot measure,
But the least motion which they made
It seemed a thrill of pleasure."

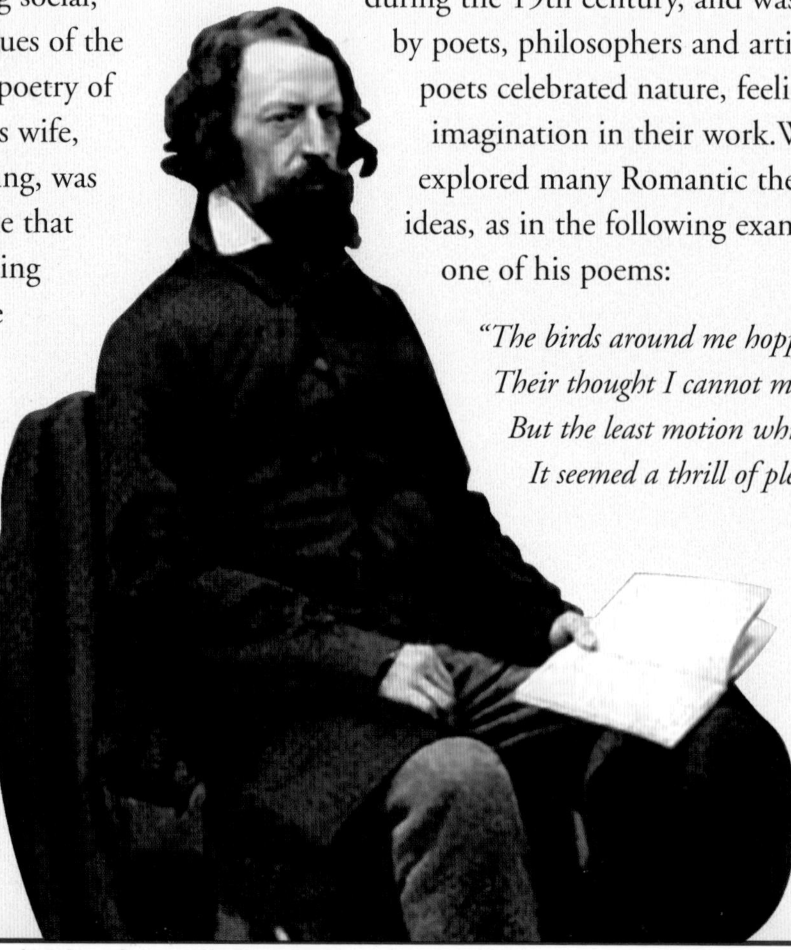

Alfred, Lord Tennyson was one of the greatest poets of the Victorian era and became Poet Laureate.

Source – Written in Early Spring, *William Wordsworth*, in Palgrave's Golden Treasury, 1875

Words to use in your project

contemporary *(happening now or in the same time period)*
epitomise *(describe something perfectly)*
interact *(communicate)*
introspective *(quiet and thoughtful)*
monologue *(long speech or piece of text by one person)*
non-conformist *(different)*
perpetual *(permanent)*

THE VICTORIAN NOVEL

The English **NOVEL** became very popular in Victorian times, particularly among the middle and upper classes. The novels of Charles Dickens were full of drama, **HUMOUR**, and accurate portrayal of the urban life of all classes. William Makepeace Thackeray was another novelist of the time, whose best-known work is *Vanity Fair*. Emily Brontë's *Wuthering Heights* was a daring book, especially for a female writer. She wrote about people experiencing strong emotions:

"I've stayed here and been beaten like a dog, abused and cursed and driven mad, but I stayed just to be near you, even as a dog."

Another important writer was Thomas Hardy, whose novels captured the spirit of times that were being lost to progress.

***A scene from Mira Nair's adaptation of Thackeray's novel* Vanity Fair.**

Source – Wuthering Heights, Emily Brontë, 1847

Literature Glossary

autobiography	*Story of the author's life*	**melancholy**	*Sad or unhappy*
conservative	*Society which has strict rules of behaviour*	**mode**	*Way or method of doing*
		Poet Laureate	*Country's official poet*
idealising	*Showing something in a perfect form*	**portrayal**	*Depiction in a work of art and literature*
lyrical	*Song written in words*	**urban**	*Towns and cities*

See also: Society 10–11; Art and Craft 20–21; Work and Leisure 24–25; At Home 28–29

CASE STUDY

The writer Lewis Carroll.

Children's Literature

Like adult fiction, children's fiction really blossomed in the Victorian era. The Romantic movement also influenced books written for children, idealising childhood and conjuring other worlds and strange creatures.

Distinguished WRITERS of children's fiction included Robert Louis Stevenson, Edward Lear and Lewis Carroll, who is best known for his classics *Alice in Wonderland* and *Alice Through the Looking Glass*. Magical writing was a welcome escape for children in a conservative society:

"Who are you?" said the caterpillar. This was not an encouraging opening for a conversation. Alice replied rather shyly: "I ... hardly know sir, just at present ..."

Many children's novels of the period are just as popular today.

Source – Alice Through the Looking Glass, Lewis Carroll.

Architecture

Before the Victorian era, architecture was generally quite simple in style. In contrast, Victorian architecture is notable for its massive scale and elaborate designs. The STYLES of classical periods provided inspiration, combined with the new technology of the Industrial Revolution. Iron was used for ORNATE railings around gardens, and some buildings even had iron frames. The people's new-found love of DESIGN led to more creative and ornate architecture, and people began to use adventurous colours on the outside of their homes.

VICTORIAN BUILDINGS

During the Victorian period there was a revival of many classical architectural styles. The Greek Revival (1825-1850) inspired the inclusion of columns. The Gothic Revival (1840 onwards) reproduced the intricate **DETAILING** of Tudor buildings. Italianate and Queen Anne styles were also popular. Many existing buildings were reconstructed to incorporate this kind of embellishment, including the Houses of Parliament, which were restored in 1840.

The mass construction of **BUILDINGS** and mass production of furniture and soft furnishings was made possible by industrialisation. However, many people were critical that these new methods created results that were too perfect, now that individual craftsmen no longer had a major role in their creation. In *Seven Lamps of Architecture*, the Victorian art and social critic John Ruskin wrote:

"Better the rudest work that tells a story or records a fact, than the richest without meaning." (section 7) and *When we build, let us think that we build forever." (section 10)."*

A significant portion of The Houses of Parliament was reconstructed during the Victorian era.

Source – 'The Lamp of Memory', Seven Lamps of Architecture, John Ruskin, 1849

Words to use in your project

artisan *(skilled manual worker)*
horticulture *(gardening)*
intricate *(elaborate)*
modernism *(new way of doing things)*
restoration *(renovating)*

GARDENS

The huge waterlilies were one of the main attractions at Kew Gardens.

During the 19th century, neatly-tended and abundant flower **GARDENS** and parks were very fashionable. An impressive garden was a reflection of refinement and status, and it required taste and planning.

For the first time, government funds were made available for the creation and upkeep of public gardens across Britain.

In 1841 the Royal Botanical Gardens at Kew opened to the public, with the striking Palm House created in 1848. This is an impressive greenhouse, 363 feet long, built to house exotic palms from all over the British Empire. For the Victorians, gardening was a way to create order and to connect with nature, but for many it was more; it was also an art form. Sir Walter Scott wrote:

"Nothing is more completely the child of art than a garden."

Source – Essay on Landscape Gardening, *Sir Walter Scott*

Architecture Glossary

abundant	*Overflowing*
dense	*Crowded together*
mass	*Large number of*
ornate	*Very decorative*
reconstruct	*Rebuild*
refinement	*Elegance*
revival	*Popularity of an old style*
rude	*Simple or basic*
vessel	*Ship*

See also: The Empire 6–7; Society 10–11; Literature 44–15; Clothes and Jewellery 22–23

CASE STUDY

A view of Tower Bridge, London.

Tower Bridge

For hundreds of years, London Bridge was the only crossing over the Thames. By the 19th century, east London was so densely populated that journeys were being delayed literally by hours, and people demanded a new crossing.
The Corporation of London agreed, but had to work out how to do this without disrupting river traffic.

The Special Bridge or Subway Committee was formed in 1876, and more than 50 designs were put forward for consideration. In 1884 a design by Horace Jones and John Wolfe Barry was chosen.
The construction of the **BRIDGE**, which opens to allow tall vessels through, took eight years. Tower Bridge was given its name because it is directly by the Tower of London.

Significant People

Some exceptional people emerged during Queen Victoria's rule, and were responsible for turning it into one of the golden eras of British history. They made a deep impact on the CULTURAL and POLITICAL life of England and their contributions to literature, art, medicine, science, architecture, transportation and politics had a lasting effect. One of the most significant legacieswas the way in which women began to be appreciated as intellectuals and achievers in their own right, though it was not until the following century that they would be allowed to vote.

FAMOUS VICTORIANS

Famous Victorians came from many walks of life. The **ENGINEER** Isambard Kingdom Brunel designed the Clifton Suspension Bridge and the Great Western Railway, and built the SS Great Eastern, the largest ship of its time. Benjamin Disraeli was Britain's first Jewish prime minister. His foreign policy played a major part in Britain's imperial expansion. He is remembered best for bringing India and the Suez Canal under control of the crown, and his political style might be summed up thus:

"Action may not always bring happiness; but there is no happiness without action".

William Gladstone held the post of prime minister four times. A religious man, he considered a career in the church before becoming a politician. David Livingstone was an explorer, cartographer and missionary who made three long **EXPLORATIONS** of East Africa. Cricketer WG Grace broke many records and made the game widely popular.

This bronze statue of Isambard Kingdom Brunel overlooks the Thames at Temple, London.

Source – speech by Benjamin Disraeli

Words to use in your project

aristocracy *(privileged class)*
domesticity *(devotion to home and family life)*
generation *(span of 20 to 30 years)*
genteel *(courteous)*
gentry *(high society)*
unique *(the only one of its kind)*

UNCONVENTIONAL WOMEN

For centuries, marriage and having children were considered the main purpose of women. During the Victorian era, many women questioned this and began to fight for the same rights as men. Elizabeth Garrett Anderson was the first British woman to qualify as a doctor. She founded a hospital for poor women and children in London. Anne Knight, who was a Quaker, took an active role in the Anti-Slavery and Temperance campaigns. She fought for the women's suffrage movements, and in 1847 published what is believed to be the first leaflet advocating the cause:

Plaque erected in London to mark the life of Elizabeth Garrett Anderson.

"Never will the nations of the earth be well governed until both sexes, as well as all parties, are fully represented, … and a hand in the enactment and administration of the laws."

Women suffragettes campaign for the right to vote.

Source – Anne Knight, leaflet published in 1847 believed to be the first call for women's suffrage

Significant People Glossary

cartographer *Map maker*
enacted *Passed (with regard to a law)*
explorations *Distant journeys*
intellectual *Great thinker*
legacy *Something handed down to future generations*
pioneer *One of the first*
Quaker *Member of the Christian Society of Friends*
sanitation *Healthy conditions*
suffrage *Right to vote*
temperance *Anti-alcohol*

See also: Victorians 4–5; Literature 14–15; Health and Medicine 26–27; Work and Leisure 24–25

CASE STUDY

Florence Nightingale

Florence Nightingale was a pioneer of NURSING and had a huge influence on improving sanitation in hospitals. Born to a wealthy family, she believed that God had called her to take up nursing, which was usually the profession of lower-class women. Nightingale and her team of 38 nurses, volunteered to tend wounded soldiers at the Crimean War (1854-56) where the lamp she carried as she comforted soldiers at night earned her the nickname "The Lady With the Lamp".

Portrait of Florence Nightingale by an unknown artist.

Florence Nightingale was the first woman awarded the British Order of Merit. Her eagerness to improve conditions in hospitals fuelled a lifelong campaign. She wrote:

"It may seem a strange principle to enunciate as the very first requirements of a hospital: that it should do the sick no harm."

Source – Notes on Hospitals, *Florence Nightingale, 1959*

Art and Craft

Art and craft in Victorian Britain has been criticised for being overly sentimental and moralistic. In truth, many artists were revolutionary, and introduced new methods, styles and purposes to their work. The many different styles of art and MUSIC that emerged catered for a wide variety of tastes and also tackled issues that were of concern at the time. During Victorian times, art began to be something that could be enjoyed by everyone, rather than just the privileged few. Photography was also widely explored and practised.

ART AND CRAFT

Various schools of art emerged during the long reign of Queen Victoria, including Clacissism, neo-Classicism, Romanticism, Impressionism, post-Impressionism and the pre-Raphaelite movement. Like novelists and poets of the period, Victorian **ARTISTS** were concerned with representing contemporary issues and ideas, and drew heavily on **SYMBOLISM**. Many artists painted idyllic landscapes and country scenes.

Classicism was heavily influenced by ancient Greek and Roman architecture. Romanticism paid tribute to emotions and feelings, often using bold, bright colours for added drama.

The pre-Raphaelite movement derived its name from its fascination with the style of art that preceded the work of Renaissance painter Raphael. The pre-Raphaelites painted people, particularly women, using methods so true to life that they often looked like photographs.

***The Mirror of Venus*, by Sir Edward Burne-Jones, was painted in 1898.**

Among many important developments of the Victorian era was the founding of many public libraries, museums and art galleries that helped to make cultural pursuits available for an increasing number of people.

Words to use in your project

aesthetic *(artistic)*
graphic *(relating to visual art)*
incorporate *(include something as part or a whole)*
masterpiece *(wonderful work of art)*
portray *(show something visually)*
reminisce *(remember past events)*
rustic *(of the country)*

MUSIC

Much of the music that the Victorians listened to, including old songs, **HYMNS** and concert music, was serious and conservative, offering views on politics and culture, or celebrating the 'golden era'.

Marie Lloyd was a popular music hall entertainer.

Operettas also became **POPULAR**, due to the unique talents of Gilbert and Sullivan. Gilbert used wit and rhyme in his lyrics, which inspired many popular 20th-century lyricists.

Music halls were well attended. **PERFORMANCES** involved lively singing and dancing, a bit like theatre, although the audience was encouraged to participate and make lots of noise. The music halls also provided opportunity for social comment, as in this song written during the 1878 Balkan crisis:

"We don't want to fight,
but by jingo if we do...
We've got the ships, we've got
the men, and we've got the
money too!"

Source – from Macdermott's War Song, *1878, by G.W. Hunt*

Art and Craft Glossary

Balkan	*Of countries in southern Europe*
by jingo	*Mild swear word*
devotion	*Commitment and dedication*
ennoble	*Give greater dignity*
idyllic	*Perfect and unspoilt*
moralistic	*Concerned with right and wrong*
operetta	*Short opera*
post-mortem	*After death*
preceded	*Came before*
Renaissance	*Art movement of the 14th-16th centuries*
revolutionary	*Ahead of its time*
symbolism	*Use of symbols to represent ideas*

See also: Religion 8–9; Architecture 16–17; Clothes and Jewellery 22–23; Work and Leisure 24–25

CASE STUDY

The Mammalian Room ***is from a collection of photographs by Frederick York of Notting Hill, London in 1875.***

Photography

Initially, photography was regarded not as art, but as a way of recording important events like birth, marriage and even death. Early cameras took a long time to capture an image so people who posed had to stay still for many minutes.

Victorian photographs, such as those of Julia Margaret Cameron, were responsible for transforming photography into an art form. She said:

"My aspirations are to ennoble photography and to secure it for the character and uses of high art by combining the real and ideal and sacrificing nothing of the truth by devotion to poetry and beauty."

Post-mortem photographs were also taken, especially of children, laid out fully dressed as if sleeping. These photographs were intended to comfort the bereaved relatives.

Source – Julia Margaret Cameron, Annals of my Glass House, *1874*

Clothes and Jewellery

Fashion for women ranged from simple day dresses to ELABORATE evening gowns for wealthy people. Working-class people wore plain clothing that was suitable for their lifestyle and work. Upper-class women would often change their clothes several times a day and wore clothes made from delicate fabrics and ornamented with EXPENSIVE ribbon and lace. For middle-class women, clothes were a status symbol and they copied the styles of dress worn by the upper classes.

FASHION AND COSTUME

Victorian women wore modest clothing that covered the entire body, and ankles were protected from view by boots laced right up to the top. Corsets held the figure in tight control, and a tiny waist was considered essential. No well-bred Victorian woman would venture outdoors without **GLOVES** and a **HAT**. With the mass production of artificial dyes clothes became more colourful.

Men of all classes wore trousers, a shirt and a formal coat, often with a waistcoat. Hats varied according to class: working-class men wore caps, middle class men favoured a type of hat known as a derby, and the upper classes could be seen in top hats.

Children of both sexes wore dresses up to the age of five or six, when boys were put into breeches, shirts and jackets. Sailor jackets were popular, with trousers for boys and skirts for girls. Thomas Carlyle wrote a whole book about the meaning of clothes. He said:

"The first purpose of Clothes … was not warmth or decency, but ornament.… Warmth he [the primitive human being] found in the toils of the chase; or amid dried leaves, in his hollow tree, in his bark shed, or natural grotto: but for Decoration he must have Clothes."

A lady's fan, made in about 1885.

Source – Thomas Carlyle, Sartor Resartus, 1834

Words to use in your project

accoutrements *(accessories)*
bonnet *(type of hat)*
garment *(any article of clothing)*
perfume *(fragrance or pleasing odour)*
tassel *(an ornamental tuft of threads)*

JEWELLERY

During the Victorian era, **CRAFTSMAN** jewellers including Tiffany began to emerge. They made fine jewellery of an exceptionally high standard, though only rich people could afford it. Victorian jewellery included brooches, necklaces, rings, bracelets. lockets, cameos, and hair pins and combs.

After Prince Albert's death, Queen Victoria abandoned diamonds and precious jewels in favour of items made of black jet from the Whitby area of north-east England. Others followed enthusiastically, and began a huge fashion for mourning jewellery, which was often set with a lock of the dead person's hair.

Mass production of jewellery also began, though much of it was of a low quality. Some women rebelled against these machine-made items and chose to wear no jewellery at all.

A late Victorian brooch, with a heart shaped amethyst set in a cut diamond border.

Clothes and Jewellery Glossary

adorned *Decorated*
braids *Plaits*
breeches *Trousers*
cameo *Silhouette of a person worn as jewellery*
chignon *Style in which hair is twisted at the back of the head*
gown *Dress*
magnificent *Grand, impressive*
mourning *Time of sadness after a death*
passionate *Having strong feelings*
rebelled *Decided against*
temples *Sides of the forehead*

CASE STUDY

This photograph shows an elaborate Victorian hairstyle.

Hairstyles

HAIRSTYLES for women became increasingly decorative during the course of Victoria's reign. In early Victorian times, hair was usually worn parted in the middle and pulled smooth over the temples. In the 1850s, large coils of hair were held back with black or coloured silk nets. In the 1860s, the chignon or French twist became popular, often accompanied by loops and braids of hair. False hair was often used to achieve elaborate effects, and hair was frequently adorned with jewelled bands, combs, flowers and even strings of pearls. From the 1870s, hair at the back of the head was sometimes worn loose. In the 1880s, a simpler style known as the Gibson Girl or Psyche Knot became popular and hair was swept into a high knot on top of the head.

See also: Significant People 18–19; Art and Craft 20–21; Health and Medicine 26–27; At Home 28–29

Work and Leisure

The type of work people did was divided along CLASS lines. Working-class men usually had manual jobs in places such as factories and mines, while working-class women were EMPLOYED as maids, factory workers and also in mines. Middle-class men worked as bankers, clerks and in various office jobs; middle-class women worked as secretaries and governesses. The upper classes, however, created whole lifestyles around SOCIAL visits and other idle pursuits; literally, hunting, shooting and fishing.

HARD LABOUR

At the start of the Victorian era, working conditions in mills, factories and industrial plants were dire. There were no unions, and people had to work extremely long hours with few breaks. Working **CONDITIONS** were often dreadful. Some miners were exposed to toxic gases and subjected to back-breaking physical labour, without any kind of protective equipment. Both men and women worked the mines, and in 1842 a Royal Commission was set up to investigate conditions. One woman told it:

"I have a belt round my waist and a chain passing between my legs, and I go on my hands and feet. The road is very steep, and we have to hold by a rope, and where there is no rope, by anything we can catch hold of... I am not as strong as I was, and cannot stand the work as well as I used to..."

The MP Lord Shaftesbury was dedicated to improving working conditions in factories and mines. He was particularly committed to protecting the rights of child workers, many of whom were subjected to the same conditions as adult workers.

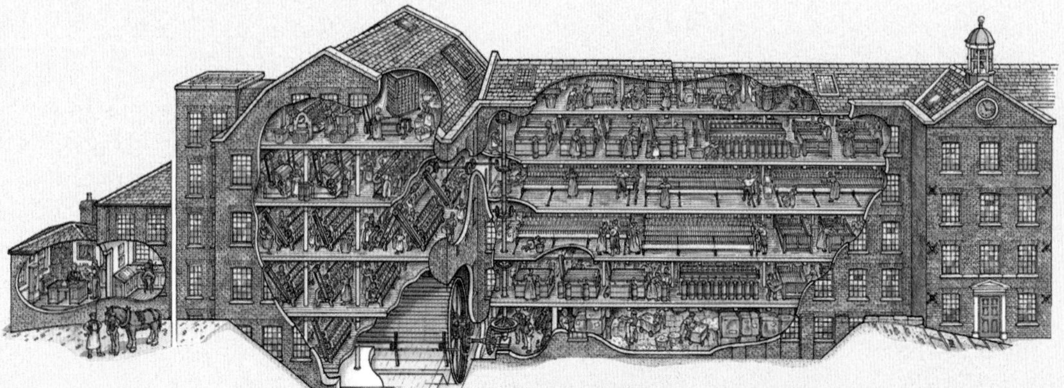

Victorian Britain saw the emergence of great factories such as this cotton mill at Quarry Bank near Manchester.

Source – Betty Harris, drawer in a coal mine, to the Royal Commission on Mines, 1842

Words to use in your project

excursion *(pleasure trip)*
exploitation *(taking advantage of someone or something)*
industrious *(hard-working)*
legislation *(law)*
recreation *(fun)*
refreshments *(food and drink)*

THE GROWTH OF LEISURE

Despite the long hours they worked, Victorians had more leisure time than ever before. Reading, music and the arts were favourite pastimes, and **THEATRES** and **MUSIC HALLS** were particularly popular. Technological advances led to the emergence of the cinema, which was an immediate hit with the public. Favourite **SPORTS** included croquet and cricket. Board games were also popular.

Victorian prime minister and popular novelist Benjamin Disraeli said:

"Increased means and increased leisure are the two civilizers of man".

Portrait of W.G. Grace *by Archibald James Stuart, painted in 1890.*

Source – Benjamin Disraeli, from a speech given in Manchester, 1872

Work and Leisure Glossary

croquet *Gentle game played with mallet and balls*
dire *Very bad*
emergence *Beginning*
idle *Slow and relaxed*
leisure *Free time*
mine *Underground works where coal and precious metals are gathered*
pursuits *Hobbies*
refinement *Elegant behaviour*
silverware *Tableware made of silver*
toxic *Poisonous*
union *Organisation that represents workers' rights*

See also: The Empire 6–7; Society 10–11; Literature 14–15; Art and Craft 20–21

CASE STUDY

Afternoon tea for a middle-class Victorian family.

Afternoon Tea

The ceremony of afternoon tea took place daily in most middle- and upper-class homes. It is reputed to date from about 1840, when an English Duchess made a habit of ordering tea and cakes in the afternoon. It soon became a symbol of refinement. In upper-class homes, high tea was an occasion when servants would pour the tea for guests, using only the finest silverware and crockery.

The politician William Gladstone described the importance of tea for the Victorians:

"If you are cold, tea will warm you. If you are too heated, it will cool you. If you are depressed, it will cheer you. If you are excited, it will calm you."

Source – William Gladstone, 1865

Health and Medicine

As the population grew, so did the spread of DISEASES. Advances in science meant that the TREATMENT available for various conditions improved. The introduction of antiseptic meant that fewer people died from infectious diseases, after operations, and in childbirth. Queen Victoria became the first member of the Royal family to use the newly-developed anaesthetic for pain relief when she had a baby. The average life span increased as medical care and sanitation improved.

DISEASES

Many diseases were common in the 19th century, but several of these produced the same **SYMPTOMS** of **FEVER**, headache, coughing, and vomiting. Epidemics of cholera and typhoid caused thousands of deaths, and people living in damp, unheated houses often contracted the lung disease tuberculosis. Most diseases affected people of all ages, but some that seemed to affect children in particular included chickenpox, diphtheria, measles, mumps, scarlet fever, whooping cough and poliomyelitis (also known as polio), all of which could be fatal. People had to pay to see a doctor so most illnesses were treated by a mother at home.

Everyone had their own home cures. Some people thought you could prevent colds by sewing children into brown paper vests smeared with thick lard. They kept them on all winter. Mrs. Isabella Beeton in her book of Household Management wrote about the various precautions to be taken especially for children to protect them from diseases:

"We see elaborate care bestowed on a family of children, everything studied that can tend to their personal comfort,— pure air, pure water ... despite of all this care and vigilance, disease and death invading the guarded treasure".

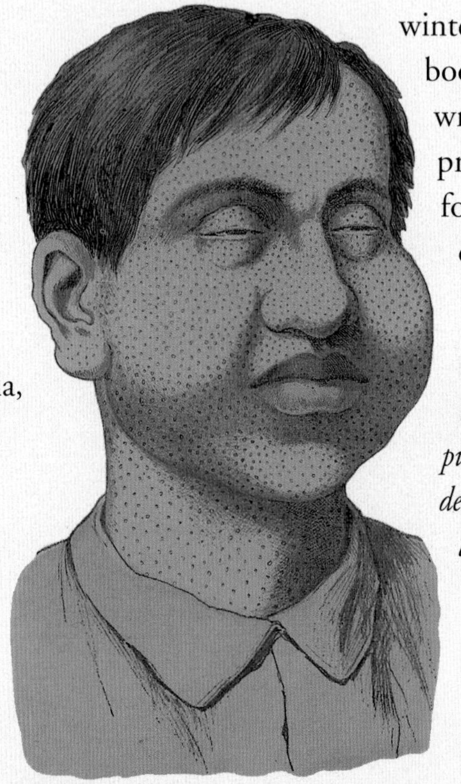

This cartoon shows an unfortunate man suffering from smallpox. The disease was a major killer, along with typhoid and cholera.

Source – The Book of Household Management by *Isabella Beeton*

Words to use in your project

anatomy *(study of the body)*
epidemic *(rapid spread of a contagious disease)*
gruelling *(exhausting)*
practitioner *(someone who practises)*
prescription *(medicine suggested by a doctor)*
primitive *(age old or ancient)*

MEDICAL PRACTICES

Healthcare in early Victorian times was often poor and most medicine was of little or no help. Little was known about the cause of disease, let alone its cure. Many doctors were poorly-trained, found it difficult to diagnose diseases effectively, and had limited ways to treat patients. They did not understand the causes of disease, so they treated only the symptoms. If, for example, a person had a rapid heartbeat, a doctor might give **MEDICINE** to slow the heart rate, but could not cure the cause. This was advice given on treating inflamed tonsils, which the Victorians called 'hospital throat':

"If taken at once, a 'hospital throat' can generally be cured by a simple gargle, chlorate of potash, port wine and vinegar, or even plain water... I saw a case of this kind, which looked very threatening, cured in one night by a very simple remedy: a gargle of brown sugar and vinegar ... and a linseed poultice put round the neck before going to bed".

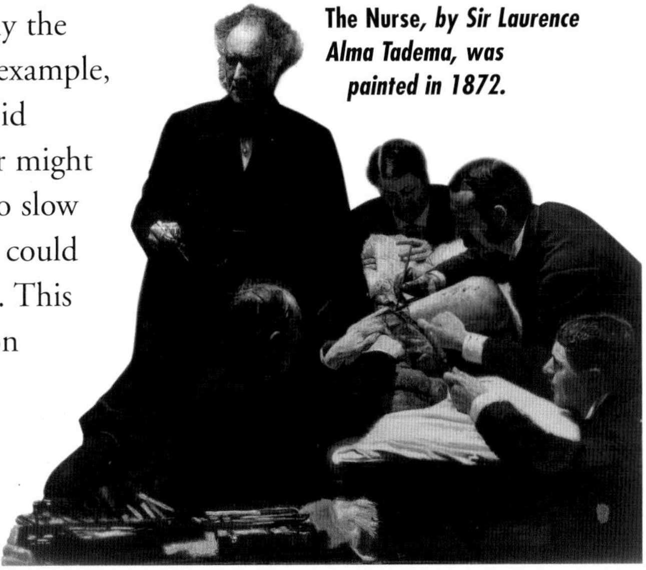

The Nurse, *by Sir Laurence Alma Tadema, was painted in 1872.*

Source – *'A Few Hints on Health and Nursing'*, in The Girl's Own Annual, *1885*

Health and Medicine Glossary

anaesthetic	*Substance that numbs pain*
antiseptic	*Something that kills germs*
epidemic	*Disease caught by lots of people*
fallacy	*Wrong belief*
gargle	*To wash the throat with a liquid*
lard	*Animal fat*
poultice	*Hot mixture spread on the skin*
sanitation	*Healthy conditions*
smeared	*Covered with*
symptom	*Sign of disease*

See also: Victorians 4–5; Education 12–13; Significant People 18–19; Trade and Transport 30–31

CASE STUDY

Home Remedies

The majority of people in the Victorian age depended on traditional remedies or herbal **CURES**. Folk remedies were not entirely useless, however. As medical science has advanced, experts have realised that herbs and traditional cures can sometimes work.

Health advice was also obtained from household manuals. It was often out of date, even compared to the limited medical knowledge of the era. Almost any minor illness was diagnosed as a cold and treated as such.

Nearly all manuals blamed the majority of illnesses on bad air and bad smells. Florence Nightingale criticised this practice. She wrote:

"Another extraordinary fallacy is the dread of night air. What air can we breathe at night but night air? ... An open window most nights in the year will never hurt any one."

This painting* The Mission of Mercy, *made in 1856 by Jerry Barrett, shows Florence Nightingale tending wounded soldiers.

Source – Notes on Nursing, Florence Nightingale, 1860

At Home

The homes of wealthy Victorians were large and surrounded by gardens, sometimes with an ESTATE that covered a large area. The growing middle-class population lived in large, comfortable town houses, decorated in the latest style. Poor people lived in overcrowded tenement buildings or small houses in CRAMPED conditions, often sharing toilets and a water pump. Conditions for the poor improved during the 19th century thanks to a number of government and local initiatives which led to cities becoming cleaner places.

HOUSES

More people moved into the **TOWNS** and **CITIES** of Britain to find work in factories. London, like most cities, was unprepared for this great increase in people. People packed into already crowded buildings, and whole families lived in single rooms. Private landlords built rows of small, cheap, brick houses to rent out. There was no indoor sanitation and a whole street might share a few outside toilets and a pump. Water from the pump was frequently polluted, and it is no surprise that many children did not survive to adulthood.

A typical Victorian house in Ironbridge, Shropshire.

The homes of the middle and upper classes were better built, larger and often incorporated the latest gadgets installed, including gas lighting, inside bathrooms and flushing toilets. These houses were decorated in the latest style, with heavy curtains, flowery wallpaper, carpets and rugs, ornaments, well- made furniture, paintings and plants. These houses often had housekeepers to take care of the household affairs. Isabella Beeton wrote:

"... where there is a house steward, the housekeeper must consider herself as the immediate representative of her mistress, and bring, to the management of the household, all those qualities of honesty, industry, and vigilance, in the same degree as if she were at the head of her own family."

***Source* – The Book of Household Management by Isabella Beeton**

Words to use in your project

enclosure *(area of land surrounded by a fence or walls)*
gadgets *(mechanical devices)*
lodgings *(a place to live in)*
prohibit *(refuse to allow; ban)*
sanitary *(healthy hygienic condition)*
tax *(money paid to the government)*

COOKING AND CLEANING

All major household chores were done by hand. Laundry was washed in a copper pot, put through a mangle to remove water, then dried on a line. Ironing took hours because the iron had to be heated repeatedly over a fire. Shopping for food and preparing everything by hand also took up a lot of time. Cooking was done over an open fire or in a range cooker heated by wood or solid fuel. The fire in a kitchen range was put out each night, so every morning it had to be cleaned, rubbed with black lead paste, polished and lit. Food was stored in larders or in refrigerators towards the end of the Victorian era.

A Victorian refrigerator, of about 1900.

In poor families **CHILDREN** had to help with the household chores, while better-off families employed at least one servant, often a young 'maid of all work'.

At Home Glossary

cramped	*Crowded*
ghastly	*Horrible*
in all conscience	*By any standard*
larder	*Cool cupboard*
mangle	*Set of rollers used to remove water from laundry*
polluted	*Dirty*
sanitation	*Measures designed to produce hygienic conditions*
tenement	*Buildings divided into rooms to rent*
vigilance	*Careful watch*

See also: Religion 8–9; Architecture 16–17; Art and Craft 20–21; Work and Leisure 24–25

CASE STUDY

Urban Life

At the start of the Victorian era people were either rich or poor. Then the middle classes developed. Everyone hoped for a better LIFESTYLE. Families with money seemed determined to acquire more, and to make their wealth obvious. Servants were useful and seen as status symbols. Health improved as a comprehensive system of sanitation, including city sewers, pumping stations and even public baths was put in place. Even so, it seemed that many poor people were sinking further into degradation. In 1889 George Sims wrote about urban life for the poor:

"More than one-fourth of the daily earnings of the citizens of the slums goes over the bars of the public-houses and gin-places... that is a fact ghastly enough in all conscience..."

Only rich households had indoor flushing toilets.

Source – Horrible London, George Sims, 1889

Trade and Transport

Transport developed very rapidly during the Victorian era. There was an increased need for better methods of MOVING goods. The changes to the transport system came in several STAGES. First ROADS were improved, then CANALS were built and finally railways were developed. Each change had its own impact on life in the country, shortening the time taken to travel long distances, and allowing goods to be sent to new markets in areas of the country that were previously out of reach.

TRADING

Tea clippers were an effective form of transport for international trade.

In the 19th century, Britain led the world in trade, and its **MERCHANT** navy carried goods all round the globe. In the mid-1850s, exports to Asia were worth more than £20 million. In 1848 Britain produced half the world's pig-iron, and over the next 30 years that output trebled. Britain's foreign trade was more than that of France, Italy and Germany put together.

Overseas investment was vital to the nation's prosperity. The City of London quickly became the centre of the financial world. Service industries expanded and began to dominate trade. Other important trade goods included cotton and other textiles from Britain's colonies, and machine tools developed in Manchester. With Britain's **FLOURISHING** trade came unrest from dock workers who demanded higher wages. Chairman of the Dock Directors, a Mr S Holland, said:

"What the cost would be of granting the demands of the men, I cannot exactly say, but it would be at least £100,000 and that would mean we should have to raise our rates. We cannot afford an advance in wages, for it would either destroy any possibility of dividend to the shareholders of the joint companies or tend to drive shipping from the port. When the pinch comes, as come it must, the hopes of the strikers will receive a severe shock and I shall be surprised if there is any backbone left."

Source – Manchester Evening News, August 16, 1889

Words to use in your project

combustion *(the process of burning)*
ingenious *(cunning)*
magnitude *(extent)*
signal *(sign)*
stagecoach *(horse-drawn coach)*
standardise *(to regulate)*
suburban *(beyond the city limits)*

TRANSPORTATION

y 1852, all Britain's main rail routes ad been built, and **PASSENGERS** and oods could be transported quickly and asily. Train travel was far cheaper than ther forms of transport, for those brave nough to try it. The writer Thomas Carlyle described his first journey:

I was dreadfully frightened before he train started; it seemed to ne certain that I should faint, from the impossibility of getting the horrid thing stopped."

In towns, people used horse-drawn buses. In the country, wagons carried people, goods and animals. Wealthy people had horses and carriages. In 1865, the first petrol driven 'horseless carriage' appeared. In 1885 the 'safety bicycle', with two equal-sized wheels, was introduced and the new pastime of cycling in the country was discovered by the rich.

One of the strange inventions of the era was the steam bicycle.

Source – Thomas Carlyle, from Letters and Memorials of Jane Welsh Carlyle, 1941.

Trade and Transport Glossary

enormous	*Of great size*
financial	*Related to money matters*
flourishing	*Prospering*
granting	*Agreeing to allow*
horrid	*Unpleasant*
investment	*Money-making scheme*
lucrative	*Producing money or profit*
pig-iron	*Iron made in moulds that look a bit like pigs*
restrictions	*Limitations*
substantial	*Sturdy*
shareholders	*Owners of shares in a company*

See also: The Empire 6–7; Clothes and Jewellery 22–23; Health and Medicine 26–27; At Home 28–29

CASE STUDY

This Owen Jones watercolour,* The Great Exhibition, *was painted in 1851.

The Great Exhibition

Queen Victoria's husband Prince Albert dreamed up the idea of a world fair. It was to be a showcase for the industrial achievements of Britain and the other nations invited to take part. After two years of planning, the Great Exhibition opened in London's Hyde Park on May 1, 1851. Its centrepiece was a huge glass building, designed by Joseph Paxton. More than six million people from all over the country and overseas came to see more than 14,000 EXHIBITS. The Poet Laureate Alfred, Lord Tennyson wrote:

***"...Steel and gold, and corn and wine,
Fabric rough or fairy-fine, ...a feast
Of wonder, out of West and East,
...All of beauty, all of use,
That one fair planet can produce..."***

When it closed in September, Paxton's 'Crystal Palace' was dismantled and re-erected on a site in Sydenham, London, where it stood for more than 80 years until it was destroyed by fire.

Source – Lines written to commemorate the Great Exhibition by Alfred, Lord Tennyson.

Index

VICTORIAN TIMELINE

1832
The Reform Act grants more men the right to vote and gives more MPs to the big cities. Parliament becomes more representative.

1833
The Factory Reform Act makes it illegal to employ children under nine in factories and limits the hours older children can work.

1837
Queen Victoria comes to the throne, aged 18. Isambard Kingdom Brunel builds the first passanger steamship to cross Atlantic.

1840
Victoria marries Prince Albert.

1847
Vanity Fair *by William Thackeray and* Wuthuring Heights *by Emily Brontë are published. Anne Knight proposes that women are given the vote. Chloroform is used as an anaesthetic.*

1848
Pre-Raphaelite movement begins.

1850
Most railway lines in Britain have been built by this date.

1851
The Great Exhibition opens.

1854–56
The Crimean War. Florence Nightingale improves conditions in the hospitals.

1859
Charles Darwin publishes The Origin of the Species*, his theory of evolution.*

1861
Prince Albert dies.

1865
Elizabeth Garrett Anderson becomes the first woman to qualify as a doctor.

1867
The Reform Act gives working men the right to vote, although the very poorest men are still excluded.

1868
The leader of the Liberal Party, William Gladstone, becomes Prime Minister for the first time.

1874
Benjamin Disraeli becomes Prime Minister.

1876
Queen Victoria is crowned Empress of India.

1880
William Gladstone becomes Prime Minister. The Education Act is passed, making school compulsory for all children aged 5–10.

1882
Married Women's Property Act allows women to continue to own the property they held before marriage.

1901
Queen Victoria dies.

***PICTURE CREDITS:* Bridgeman Art Library: 20, 21c, 25c, 26, 27 all, 31r. Corbis: 16-17 all, 18, 29 all, 30. Curios Photo Library: 22, 23c. Features Art Library: 4, 5, 6, 8, 9c, 10, 12, 13c. London Photo Library: 7br, 9r, 11 all, 14, 15r, 19 all, 21r, 23r, 25r. London Transport Library: 7t, 31c. Rex Features: 15c.**